Mighty Machines

BULLDOZERS

by Amanda Doering Tourville
illustrated by Zachary Trover

Content Consultant:
Paul M. Goodrum, PE, PhD, Associate Professor
Department of Civil Engineering, University of Kentucky

wagon

visit us at www.abdopublishing.com

Published by Magic Wagon, a division of the ABDO Group, 8000 West 78th Street, Edina, Minnesota, 55439. Copyright © 2009 by Abdo Consulting Group, Inc. International copyrights reserved in all countries. All rights reserved. No part of this book may be reproduced in any form without written permission from the publisher.

Looking Glass Library™ is a trademark and logo of Magic Wagon.

Printed in the United States.

Text by Amanda Doering Tourville
Illustrations by Zachary Trover
Edited by Patricia Stockland
Cover and interior design by Emily Love

Library of Congress Cataloging-in-Publication Data
Tourville, Amanda Doering, 1980-
  Bulldozers / by Amanda Doering Tourville ; illustrated by Zachary Trover.
      p. cm. — (Mighty machines)
  Includes index.
  ISBN 978-1-60270-621-7
  1. Bulldozers—Juvenile literature. I. Trover, Zachary, ill. II. Title.
  TA735.T6887 2009
  629.225—dc22
                              2008035996

Table of Contents

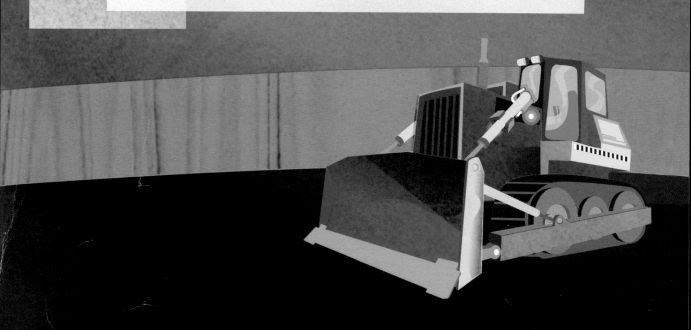

What Are Bulldozers?

Bulldozers are machines that move earth. A bulldozer pushes away dirt or rock to leave a flat surface.

A blade, two hydraulic arms, two tracks, an engine, and a cab make up a bulldozer. Some bulldozers have rippers, too.

Parts of Bulldozers

A bulldozer's main tool is a blade. The blade is mounted on the front of the machine. It is made of strong steel, so it won't bend or break.

The edges of the blade are curved. This curve helps keep the dirt or rock together as it is pushed.

Two hydraulic arms are connected to the blade. These arms move and tilt the blade. Liquid in the arms creates pressure. This moves the arms up and down. The bulldozer operator controls these arms with a lever.

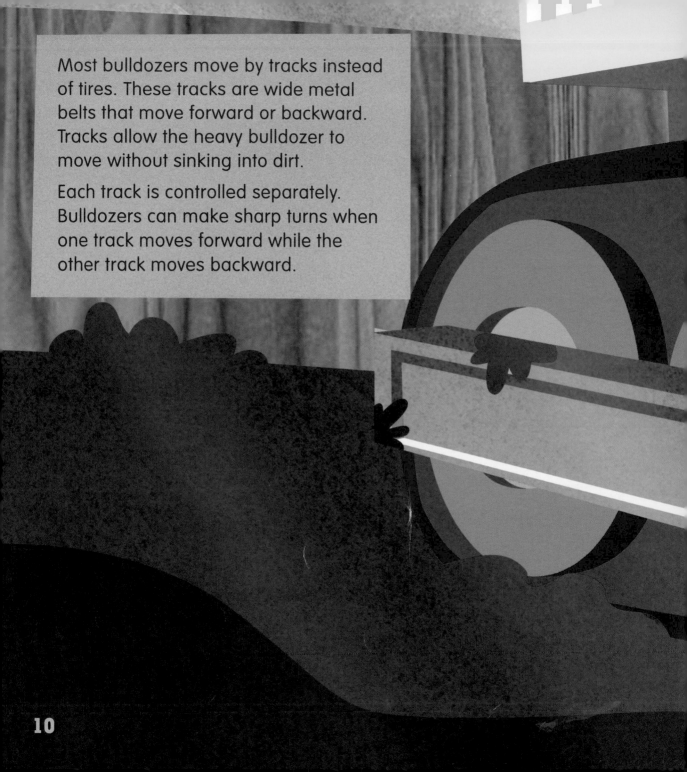

Most bulldozers move by tracks instead of tires. These tracks are wide metal belts that move forward or backward. Tracks allow the heavy bulldozer to move without sinking into dirt.

Each track is controlled separately. Bulldozers can make sharp turns when one track moves forward while the other track moves backward.

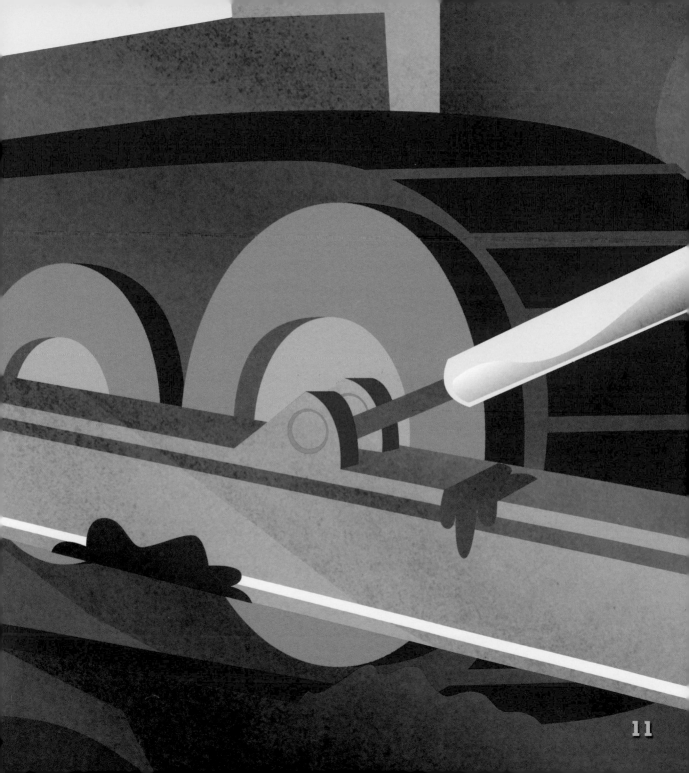

Some bulldozers have a tool called a ripper. The ripper is mounted on the back of the bulldozer. It is made of metal spikes that dig into the ground. The ripper loosens soil. It can even break up concrete.

13

14

The engine sits inside the bulldozer. It makes the bulldozer run. Large bulldozers have large engines. Small bulldozers have smaller engines. Water cools down the engine when it gets hot.

In the cab, there are several levers and foot pedals. The operator uses these levers and pedals to move the bulldozer and lift the blade.

The monitor shows the operator how much fuel is left. It also shows the temperature of the other liquids that help the bulldozer run.

How Are Bulldozers Used?

Bulldozers are used in many ways. They are mostly used at construction sites. They are usually the first machines on a new site.

Construction workers use bulldozers to break up rocks and hard dirt. Then, they use bulldozers to push and scrape the earth. This makes a flat surface on which to build.

Road construction workers use bulldozers to spread gravel to make a new road. Miners use bulldozers to move coal in coal mines. Bulldozers can also be used in demolition. They help tear down old buildings.

Where Are Bulldozers Used?

Bulldozers are used all over the world. Wide tracks allow them to work in swamps. Some bulldozers can even work in deep water, such as oceans, rivers, and lakes. Operators control the machine with a remote so they don't have to go in the water.

Foresters use bulldozers to cut down trees or remove tree stumps.

Many militaries use bulldozers in war zones. These bulldozers are protected with thick metal armor. The cab is fitted with special glass that won't break.

Bulldozers Are Mighty Machines!

Bulldozers are an important part of construction. They break up hard dirt and concrete. They push earth so that the ground is flat for building. Once bulldozers have done their jobs, other machines can construct new buildings and roads.

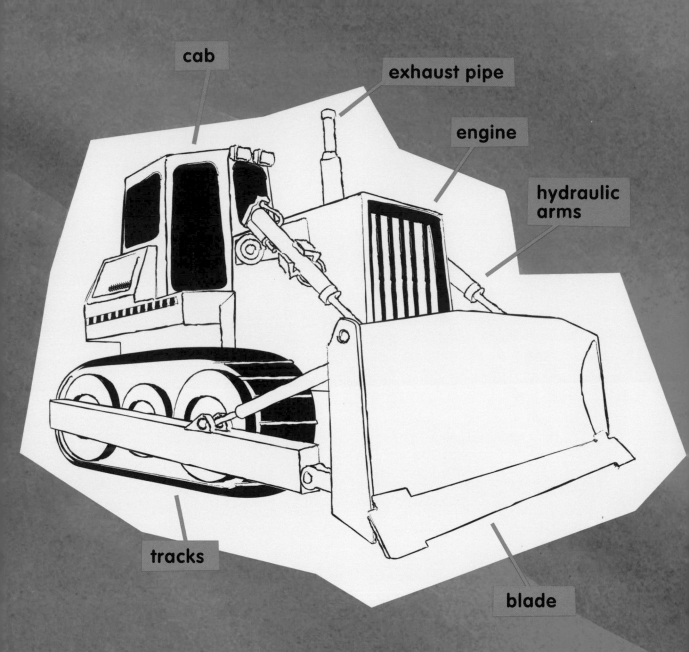

cab

exhaust pipe

engine

hydraulic arms

tracks

blade

Bulldozer Parts

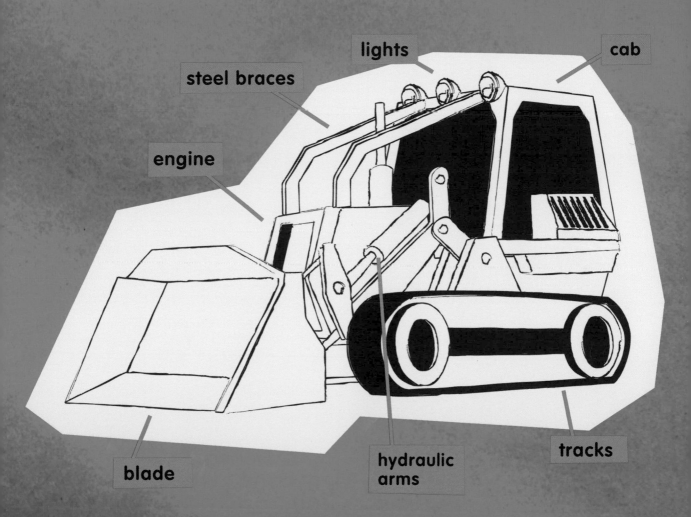

lights

cab

steel braces

engine

blade

hydraulic
arms

tracks

Fun Facts

⚙ There are several ideas about how the bulldozer was named. Some people think it was named because it is large and noisy, like a bull. Others believe the name came from the old phrase "bull dosing," which meant giving a very large dose of medicine. By the late 1800s, bulldozing meant using force to push through anything.

⚙ The first bulldozer blade was pushed by mules or horses.

⚙ Trimming dozers are used in the bellies of large ships. They gather rock, steel, or other materials with a special blade.

⚙ The first bulldozers did not have hydraulic arms to lift the blade up and down. This had to be done by hand with a crank.

⚙ Bulldozers were used in World War II to flatten the ground for troops.

⚙ Some bulldozers have tires instead of tracks. These bulldozers are mostly used for mining.

Glossary

armor—an outer layer of material that protects.

construction—the act of building or making something.

demolition—the act of destroying or tearing down something.

gravel—small pieces of rock.

hydraulic—operated or moved by liquid.

monitor—a display screen.

mount—to join an object to a support.

tilt—to move into a slanted position.

Web Sites

To learn more about bulldozers, visit ABDO Group online at **www.abdopublishing.com**. Web sites about bulldozers are featured on our Book Links page. These links are routinely monitored and updated to provide the most current information available.

Index